Enjoy Your Thoughts 101 Awakened Daughters from Conscious Mothers

Megan Elizabeth Gray

Copyright © Megan Elizabeth Gray, 2021

All rights reserved. No part of this book may be reproduced without written permission of the copyright owner except if citation is made to the book and author.

INSPIRATION

"I am an artist at living. My work of art is my Life."
-D. T. Suzuki

"Your vibe attracts your tribe."
-Anonymous

"Blessed are the curious for they shall have adventures."
-L. Drachman

"With each new day comes new strength and new thoughts."
-Eleanor Roosevelt

DEDICATION

I dedicate this book to my husband, Jamie, who gives me the space to be my truest self, makes me laugh, and supports me at every turn. Thank you for creating Lily with me.

EXPRESSION OF GRATITUDE

    I am eternally grateful to the many people whose words and insights I have absorbed over the last year during my maternity leave, and in particular: Oprah Winfrey, Susie Moore, Dr. Edith Eger, Marie Forleo, Glennon Doyle, Brené Brown, Bethany Webster, Leymah Gbowee, Cheryl Strayed, Robin Sharma, Elizabeth Gilbert, Cathy Heller, Susan Jeffers, Dr. Shefali Tsabary, Gabrielle Bernstein, Dr. Maya Angelou, Caroline Myss, Gary Zukav, Ken Robinson, Buchi Emecheta, Wes Moore, Amandla Stenberg, Father Richard Rohr, Wendy von Oech, Anaïs Nin, Paulo Coelho, Victor E. Frankel, Marianne Williamson, Malala Yousafzai, Priyanka Chopra Jonas, Tara Westover, Byron Katie, Shaka Senghor, Eckhart Tolle, Laverne Cox, Dr. Gary Chapman, Maria Konnikova, Daniel H. Pink, Rep. John Lewis, Iyanla Vanzant, Nir Eyal, Peter Diamandis, Steven Kotler, Sister Joan Chittister, Esther Perel, and Sarah Ban Breathnach. And to my own personal teachers and guides whom I believe are true angels in my life. Thank you from my whole heart.

IMPORTANT NOTE

I feel it is extremely important to state that I have written this book from my own personal experience. I am an able-bodied white woman who grew up in a relatively safe and secure neighbourhood in America and in a family that was able to afford all necessities plus a few luxuries. I, unquestionably, have benefited from, and continue to benefit from, privilege, including privilege of which I am not aware. I acknowledge that I have limitations and state that I am committed to continuing to push social progress in a way that dismantles the insidious racism, sexism, homophobia, classism, ableism, and ageism that permeates our society. I welcome any feedback on how my privilege has played out in this book; I value and appreciate being able to learn and expand my knowledge and perspective in this regard. Thank you.

FOREWORD

At the time of writing, my maternity leave is less than two weeks from being over. My daughter, Lily, is almost 13 months old. And I – I have survived.

From the moment I first held my sweet baby in my arms until this moment, I have been collecting and reflecting on thoughts I wish to share with her. I realized, as I started putting pen to paper, that I would love to share these thoughts with all daughters, and so began this book.

There is a belief that when a woman gives birth, she actually gives birth to two souls: her baby and herself, again. I believe this has been true for me. Since becoming a mom, I have grown and changed and transformed – and have fallen into many deep, dark holes – until I slowly, very slowly, began to emerge again, renewed. I credit my journey to the angels and healers along my path who filled my mind with beautiful new thoughts, insights, hope, and wisdom. Their voices and teachings remain imprinted on my heart and etched in my soul. This book captures what I have learned and what I want to share.

I have faith that in releasing this book, my energy and voice will contribute to raising our collective consciousness, and inspire you to use your energy and voice to do the same. Once we become more conscious, there is no going back: we will only become more and more conscious. My hope and prayer is for all daughters to be awakened – to have the freedom to speak their truth, speak it loud, and be their most authentic selves. Just know I am here, energetically lifting you up and lovingly encouraging you to stretch your wings, and fly.

ENJOY YOUR LIFE

The title of this book captures the best piece of advice I was ever given. My husband Jamie and I were living in Hong Kong for a year, and it was a week or so before returning to the UK. I had become totally absorbed in the Pure yoga studio a few minutes' walk from our apartment. I was decently pregnant with Lily by then, but remained committed to my practice, perhaps more than ever. My yoga teachers, in some ways, were the closest I had to friends in our Hong Kong life. I worked extremely hard as a corporate lawyer and any respite I had I spent with Jamie, ideally on the beach or exploring a new country in Asia, which didn't leave much time for socializing. I was okay with that; the connection my yoga teachers and fellow classmates provided felt enough for me. There were a few teachers whose classes I returned to week after week.

As I walked out of vinyasa 1 with Arun that day, I knew it would be my last before leaving Hong Kong. I felt timid to speak to Arun: we often smiled, and I regularly thanked him for class, but we never actually conversed. As we floated down the hall toward the locker rooms, feeling the post-yoga airy lightness, I said to him, gently, "Arun, I wanted to say goodbye to you. I am leaving Hong Kong to go back to the UK." He looked at me, with such kindness in his eyes and a slight smile on his face. I don't remember now anything he said back to me except for this: "Enjoy your life."

I walked the few minutes home feeling like I walked into a new dimension. It was a dimension in which I would, forevermore, give intentional thought to enjoying my life, and not only experience this as a by-product of other actions or intentions. It was so simple, and yet so profound. I knew I'd never forget his words and that I must pass them on. It is this thought I chose for the title of this book because I believe it underpins all the others. There is so much to this life, and I hope so much that you enjoy it.

PUT YOUR ENERGY OUT THERE

In all aspects of life, put your energy out there. Just keep putting your energy out there, and see what sticks. This applies to really everything – making friends, meeting a significant other, finding a home, looking for a job. Your energy will interact with others' energies on both conscious and subconscious levels, and you will be attracted to and connected with people who vibrate on your energy level. I believe this is the deep meaning behind the beautiful quote, *"Your vibe attracts your tribe."* This is why it feels so amazing to be with people who you feel really get you, and why it can feel lonely, even when you're in the company of other people, who you feel really do not get you.

I was thinking about putting my energy out there when I was interviewing for a new job during my maternity leave: as much as I wanted this particular job, I felt very zen about putting my energy out there during the interview process, reflecting my truest self, with faith that if it resonates and feels like a good fit, I would be hired – and, if not, that is also okay. I, possibly for the first time in my life, didn't feel like I needed to try to "control" the outcome. As it turned out, I felt an alignment with the company and my interviewers and I believe they felt it too, and, to my delight, I was offered the job.

I am passing this on to you as well: put your gorgeous, unique, powerful energy out there, and see where, with an open mind and heart, it takes you.

SPEAK YOUR TRUTH

Please don't ever feel you have to change yourself, mute yourself, quiet yourself, limit yourself, shrink yourself, or be anything other than exactly who you are in order to accommodate someone else or society. Rather, speak your truth! Speak it loud! Be your most authentic self! The bravest thing a woman can do is tell the truth about her life and, through her way of being in the world, say to others, "*This* is who I am."

Remember, too, that you have a very powerful voice – use your voice and speak up. Hold, and share, your opinions. As Priyanka Chopra Jones has said, as advice given by her father, "If you don't have an opinion, what's the point of you being here?" What you have to say is valuable. The world needs to hear it. Come from a mindset of abundance, rather than scarcity, in which *all* voices and contributions are valuable. When you do this, you also empower others to use their voices and speak their truths. You raise each other up and allow each other to shine.

LOVE

As to matters of the heart, dear daughter, I say this: choose to be with someone you really *like*. Someone you *want* to be with. Someone who gets *you*. Someone who makes your soul feel *alive*.

You cannot fake or force these feelings. You will know them when you feel them. If you aren't sure, or if you have doubts which lead you to seek external support, or advice, or validation, accept that this person may not be *your* person, and move on. Do not think you need to rush to find your person. Do not think you are being choosey, or too picky, or that your compatibility threshold is too high. You will meet your person when you are meant to. I believe it is a great misery in life being with someone who is not your person. That is why you must base your choice on your feelings – on how your heart feels toward a person – and not on typical attributes such as where they went to school, what their job is, or how objectively "good looking" they are.

Your heart knows what you want, even if you try to quiet it. You can only quiet your heart for so long. One day, it will likely turn from a whisper into a roar. And you need to follow your heart's true desire for true happiness and contentment. This is a prerequisite. Do not ask anyone for advice. No one knows your heart. Ask yourself. You will know.

I also want to tell you that if you feel you're attracted to women, to men, or to both…great. Any of these options is great. Love is love, and finding love – real, genuine love – is a sacred blessing.

One final thought – I recently saw this quote and I knew I must pass it on: "*May you attract someone who speaks your language, so you don't have to spend a lifetime translating your soul.*" Amen to this.

CHANGE

There is something in our human psyche, or at least cultural psyche, that fears change. "Change is scary," we often say to ourselves and to others, perpetuating this fear. But, why? Why do we not wholeheartedly revel in change, and welcome it into our lives?

Someone recently shared with me a beautiful quote from Rumi, a Persian poet, that captures this notion perfectly, which I paraphrase as this: *"Do not resist change, even if life is turning upside down: how do you know that the side you're used to is better than the one to come?"* I love this! We may feel comfortable in the side we're used to, but there is so much possibility in the side that's coming. Embrace it. Cherish it. Honor it. Allow *yourself* to be changed in the process.

FRIENDSHIP

Throughout your life, friends are so important. So, so important. Friends are our life blood, and our windows to ourselves. They show us who we are, and were. As captured in the beautiful quote by Anaïs Nin, *"Each friend represents a world in us, a world possibly not born until they arrive, and it is only by this meeting that a new world is born."* How magical! Each friendship creates an entirely new world: of mutual growth, of shared experiences, of collective memories. The joyous memories you have with your friends can last an entire lifetime, and never fade. Friends, after all, are the family we choose for ourselves.

Friendship must be nurtured, like a plant must be watered. I have learned that people "do friendship differently" and so how *you* require a friendship to be nurtured, in order to maintain closeness, may differ from what someone else needs. You may, for example, feel you need a lot of regular contact, whereas a friend may be content with seeing you in person every few months. There is no right or wrong – only, perhaps, compatibility.

"Old friends" and "new friends" are both to be valued and cherished in their own ways. The Girl Scout song I still remember singing as a little girl summarizes this perfectly: *"Make new friends but keep the old. One is silver and the other's gold."*

You will feel blessed to maintain friendships throughout your life, to have a shared past to look back on together. During my maternity leave, I reached out to a few friends I had lost touch with. I wanted so badly to know everything about their lives that I had missed out on. From what I've seen, it is often never too late to reconnect: a friendship of like-minded souls can be replanted in new soil, and continue to bloom.

And…if you feel you and a friend have grown apart, that is also okay. You can honor the friendship for what it was, for the time you had it. As the adage says, *"some friends are for a reason; some friends are for a season."*

Lastly, always be open to the possibility of making a new friend. I met Tessa, one of Lily's godmothers, at a work summer party when I overheard her talking and knew I wanted to talk to her. We talked for two straight hours that night. You never know when or where you could meet a friend when your heart is open to it.

KINDNESS TOWARD OTHERS

Be kind to other people. All people. Every single day, find ways to be kind to other people, such as going out of your way for someone, or lending a helping hand. Every single day. You could even make a list of the kind deeds you did or you could share them with friends or family over dinner. This is not a way to brag or make yourself feel good, but as a reminder and log of what goodness you are adding to our world.

Much of the first draft of this book I wrote by hand, in my journal, with a blue pen I loved so much that, as I was filling out pre-treatment paperwork, I asked my physiotherapist, whom I was seeing for post-pregnancy pains, if I could keep it. He said yes; as I was putting the used pen in my bag, he took out another one to give me – "You need a new one," he said, smiling. Unprovoked kindness is such a beautiful and powerful force. We must always pay kindness forward. When someone offers you kindness, in particular, look for how you can offer it to someone else. Always be on the lookout for what kindness you can contribute to our world.

REJECTING WHAT'S NOT RIGHT FOR YOU

There may come a time in your life when you are asked to do something that you feel is not right for you. You may feel a sense of "pressure" around it, or maybe not. Just know that there is power and beauty in saying no. For example, you could say: "This doesn't work for me, and I will not accept what's not right for me." This kind of gracious forthrightness is modelling for all women how to stand your ground, and not back down or be forced into something.

I felt this way, distinctly, as I was attempting to negotiate a "flexible" working arrangement for my return from maternity leave. I had requested to work fixed hours (i.e., 9am-5pm) rather than the 24/7 nature to which I had grown accustomed over the prior 10 years. I didn't feel my "old" way of working was compatible with my "new" life as a mom (which is an incredibly and entirely personal choice), and felt this arrangement would enable me to be a hardworking, dedicated corporate lawyer during work hours, and a hardworking, dedicated mom during mom hours. Unfortunately, my firm disagreed, saying that to do so would be incompatible with my job, and that if I did so I would have "no value." It upset me, on many levels. I felt sad for myself, of course, but worse for all women and the enduring state of the patriarchy which, I believe, creates resistance to change. My goal and aim and wish and prayer is that, by the time Lily is my age, she and all women will have the freedom and ability to design their lives based entirely on their own choices, rather than around what workplaces are willing to accommodate, at a minimum, and, ideally, embrace.

As my friend Siobhán helped me see, though, it takes brave people to model how to stand firm and claim one's autonomy and agency. You do not have to stay in a situation and suffer. By rejecting what's not right for you, you make space to welcome what is, and create space for others to do the same. You can create positive ripple effects for all women by claiming ownership of your life and your choices.

Being rejected by my firm was the catalyst for me to look for a new job which I felt aligned to my values and my newly-envisioned purpose in life. I will never stop pushing for progress, but I learned that sometimes progress is best achieved by extricating yourself from a certain situation, regrouping around a new perspective, welcoming into your life new teachers and guides, and setting out on a reimagined path.

THE ROLE OF PARENTS

My belief in a critical role of parents has crystalized in my mind recently. Here is what I became conscious to, which I write in the first person to my daughter Lily:

My role as your mom, beautiful daughter, is to support you as you discover for yourself your unique gifts and your authentic self. This is your journey in life. I do not know what your unique gifts are, but I know that you have them and I know that the world needs them. I also know that it is your duty – yes, your duty – to share them with the world. I am here to support you – to give you space to try things on, to succeed, to fail, to learn, to grow. You are not needing to try to impress me or make me proud. I want you, instead, to work to make yourself proud. And I am here whenever you need me.

Parents, too, must also always be conscious to how, throughout their lives, they can learn (or, sometimes, unlearn) from their children as much as their children can learn from them. Children are, in particular, the best teachers about being present; they have no longing of the past or attachment to the future. I am so excited about everything Lily will teach me along our journey together.

AUTHENTICITY

Come out as an individual. Be your one-and-only, divinely created self. As they say, everyone else is already taken. Feel amazing in the knowledge that you may set people free just by living your life in a way that is authentic to you.

I loved listening to Amandla Stenberg talking about authenticity as her activism, which is an incredible sentiment. By being yourself, by being your full self, by loving yourself – this is your revolution.

Remember that the permission you may be waiting for to be yourself is not, and never is, coming. Grant yourself permission or realize that permission is not needed. It is your God-given right to be you.

By being your authentic self, you create a life authentic to you. And you can do this no matter what your background is, no matter how far apart your current reality and your dream life are, no matter how hard or impossible it may seem. You innovate. In the words of Shaka Senghor, innovation is to use the raw materials of our circumstances to create the life we envision.

As Jamie and I say to Lily in the morning, often before Jamie leaves for work, rather than tell her to "be good" or "behave": "Be yourself today!" I hope you will follow this mantra, too. Be yourself today, and every day.

RESPECT

Respect all people. Respect, especially, people different to you. Be curious about people different to you and try to learn what it is like living as them. You may likely never fully understand, and that is okay. *Trying* to understand someone else's reality is part of how we begin to break down barriers that divide us.

Similarly, respect people's choices for their lives, as you would expect respect for your choices. Each to their own. Live and let live. These are not meaningless platitudes. They are of fundamental importance. Everyone is the authority on their own life, and their journey warrants your respect. Judging someone else's choices or journey is a form of disrespect, and implies that we know better for someone than they know for themselves. Come from a place of love and acceptance; these are pillars of respect.

MISTAKES

It took me a long time to learn that mistakes are okay! Put another way, there are actually no mistakes in life, only lessons. Do not beat yourself up, or wish the mistake away. The point of life is to learn. You learn the most – in the most meaningful way – as you go through what feel like mistakes or similar, like setbacks, disappointments, or regrets. These are all guideposts on your way to finding who you are and who you will be. As Dr. Maya Angelou beautifully said, *"when you know better, you do better."* Who you are as a person – what you know and what you are capable of – is continually evolving. Your "mistakes" are part of what make you, you.

APOLOGIZING

It is inevitable that one day you will do or say something that causes someone sadness, pain, or another emotion which feels unpleasant or unwelcome for them. You may hurt someone's feelings, or break something accidentally, or show up late, or not show up at all. In all these instances, you are a big person when you take responsibility and apologize, sincerely, for it. When you apologize, when you *really* apologize, you do not try to justify or defend yourself, or in other words try to make an excuse for your behavior. After you apologize, you may be forgiven, or you may not. It is in the other person's gift whether or not to accept your apology. You'll go from there.

Remember, though, that even if, following from your actions, someone else feels upset or angry, this does not necessarily mean that you are "wrong" or that you did something "bad." That person may have been triggered by what you did, but it could be relating to something else deeper in their lives. Always be mindful of the impact of your words and actions, never intentionally try to harm, and always try to understand from someone's perspective how you may have affected them.

ACCEPTING APOLOGIES

Others may hurt you, physically, mentally, emotionally. If they want to offer an apology, consider being willing to hear it. If you do hear it, look in your heart if you will accept it. To paraphrase Oprah's wise words, forgiveness is giving up the hope that the past could be different: it's accepting the past for what it was, and using this moment to move forward.

Note, though, if you are in a relationship with someone, particularly an intimate one, in which you feel you are continually feeling hurt, and find yourself continually receiving apologies but without anything changing in line with those apologies, please find the strength and the external support to end the relationship. Unless you break the cycle by getting out, it will continue. An example of this is what women who suffer abusive partners face in a domestic violence cycle. There are many resources dedicated to helping women escape these unimaginably horrible circumstances. (I have donated the proceeds of this book to those resources.)

STRENGTH

One day you may find yourself at a crossroads or in a difficult situation where you feel you aren't "strong enough." Please know this: you are stronger than you think you are.

My strength had never been tested more than when I was in labor with Lily. I went without pain medication until I felt like the pain from contractions was a seven out of ten. I requested an epidural, and waited. The pain felt like a ten as I was asked to sit completely still in order to receive a huge needle at the base of my back (or, if I accidentally moved, risk complications, such as headaches that would last for days). I sat on my hospital bed, still as I could, tears streaming down my face from the pain, gripping Jamie's shirt collar so tightly I thought I would rip it off.

A few hours later, I pushed Lily out into the world.

I realized in those moments: I am stronger than I think I am. I know you are too.

LAUGHTER

Laughter, even a mere moment of laughter, can raise you up and fill you with good-feeling vibrations that can shift dense, heavy energy. Look always for humor in your daily interactions. Seek out people whom you find funny and who make you feel funny. Write down your "inside jokes" and things that amused you, and look back on them when you're feeling down. I looked back recently at a list of inside jokes I had with my friend Caitlin from many years ago when we worked together in Los Angeles – sure enough, despite all the time that had passed, they still brought a smile to my face and a lightness to my heart. I love being able to remember the belly laughs we had. Laughter is a potent, heavenly force in our lives.

OPEN-MINDEDNESS

Embrace being as "open-minded" as you can be! What does this mean? Be open – welcoming, inviting, curious about, interested in – to new ideas, new foods, new people, new opinions, new methods of well-being, new perspectives, new ways of being, new ways of living. Try everything! Keep trying new things throughout your life, like hobbies, foods, technologies, languages, sports, places to visit. Never be static or complacent with what you already know or have tried. There are new things to know and new things to try. Open your mind and heart to them.

HEART BREAK

Try not to be afraid of getting your heart broken. I wonder if there are humans who go through life who never get their heart broken. In some ways, I think I would feel sad for anyone who *hasn't*, which may seem strange. I think getting one's heart broken is a part of being alive! It's a part of our universal human experience. It is so, so indescribably painful, and yet… it is still a beautiful thing to know you loved someone or something so much, it had the power to break your heart. That in itself is worth a lot.

I say: love, go and love, and always, simply, hope for the best. Do not be guided by fear of "what if it doesn't work out." Your life will go as it is supposed to. It cannot go any other way than the way it goes.

DREAMING BIG

Dream big! Dream everything. Dream things no one has dreamed before. You have, within you, the power to imagine, and then create, anything. My woman-empowerment coach Michelle once told me to keep a dream journal, in order to write down my biggest and wildest dreams. There is a distinction between this and goals. Dreams are purposefully huge and extraordinary. (For me, my dreams often involve Oprah – meeting her, talking to her, sharing insights with her – or something to do with living by the sea or journeying around the world.) You do this to keep in the mindset of creation: create, create, create. You keep your imagination and mind expansive and open by creating new possibilities. Dream it! Do it!

"SUCCESS"

In the professional world I had come to know before Lily was born, "success" often seemed to be defined rather one-dimensionally, usually denoting a career with long hours, prestige, and money. The thing I came to learn is that success is, actually, whatever you believe it to be. A wonderful perspective I saw this year goes like this: *"Happiness is the new rich. Inner peace is the new success. Health is the new wealth. Kindness is the new cool."*

This also reminds me of a beautiful post I saw on LinkedIn which appeared in my newsfeed after a colleague had liked it. An executive wrote about how she called a candidate about a new job opportunity. The candidate declined, saying he had "already made it to the top." She was confused, because the new job would be a promotion. He explained he loved his exact work, he was treated with respect, he made enough money to be comfortable, he had flexibility and he never missed his kids' sports games, anniversaries, birthdays, or any other important events. A promotion meant more time, travel, and sacrifice and – for him – this was not his version of success. He already made it to the top, as defined by him.

You choose whatever success means to you. Build your life according to your own specifications. I propose this definition of success: being in love with your life!

READING

Read. Read as much as you can. As often as you can. Different voices. Different genres. Different formats. Your mind will be enriched by every single word you read. I can still remember the excitement I would feel as a child when my dad would take my sister and me to a certain bookstore to each choose a book to buy. There was so much possibility! So many books to enjoy!

During my maternity leave, I loved making time to read in a way I hadn't for many years; I can feel how much I have expanded as a person and as a spirit because of it. I encourage you, too, to be a lover of the written word from others' perspectives and experience the journey it will take you on.

QUIET TIME

Make time for quiet reflection – whether you keep a journal, or meditate, or sit outside on a nice day. When Lily was about four months, we went outside to our little backyard and laid down on the grass, looking at the beautiful blue sky and puffy white clouds. It made me realize how many years it had been since I last did that. Meditation, in particular, I believe has a particular power to fill our spirits with calm, loving energy, and bring us clarity in an unparalleled way. This is reflected in the beautiful quote by Ma Jaya Sati Bhagavati: *"Quiet the mind, and the soul will speak."*

WORDS

Words create worlds. Choose your words intentionally. You bring into existence whatever you speak. For example, if you say you are weak, you have created your own weakness. If you say your life has meaning, you have created your meaning.

You must never intentionally use words to harm another. Words have tremendous power. You can also disempower yourself through words. Think carefully when you say something like, "I have to…" or "I need to…" or "I can't…" Often, what we really mean is "I am choosing…" or "I want…" or "I am not going to…" Don't, through your words, create your reality where you are choiceless or powerless or not in full control of your life. You have the power to create anything, including through your words.

WELL-BEING

Well-being is often thought of as physical and mental well-being, and both are equally important and inextricably connected. You must take care of your whole self. If you are ever struggling, please ask for help. Therapy, for example, can be a life-altering, sacred process. It can help you sort through, and clear through, and shift, patterns and energies that may have previously been stuck, and do not serve you. You cannot heal a wound that you ignore; it will continue to cause pain and play out perniciously in your life, often in subconscious ways.

Remember that any "belief" you hold is actually just a thought you keep thinking (credit to Abraham-Hicks); you can change your thoughts, and therefore beliefs, and also your patterns of behavior and ways of being in the world, which all impact your well-being. I also encourage you to find a way to move your body that you enjoy – dancing, swimming, tennis, anything. Find what you love and make time for it. Sometimes, even if you "don't feel like it," ask yourself, "What would make me feel good?" Often, when viewed from this slightly different lens, we can motivate ourselves to partake in an activity that will elevate our mood and brighten our current existence.

JEALOUSY

Resist the temptation to be jealous of others. As it is said, run your own race. If do you feel yourself being jealous of someone, see if you can transform it into happiness and joy for that person. One soul's joy is the elevation of our collective joy.

You can also use jealousy as a positive force as a guide. Jealousy can often show you what it is you really want in life. Ask yourself, whatever it is you are jealous of, is that actually a longing of your heart for something you want to create for yourself? It often is.

LIFE STAGES

Enjoy every stage in your life, every part of your life, as you go through it. Try not to be in a rush to grow up or move onto another stage. I recently read something which said, *"One day you played outside with your friends, and you didn't realize it was the last time."* This makes me sad to think about; it makes me nostalgic for when my sister Kristen and I used to play outside with the other neighborhood kids. As we go through life, we don't always realize when we may be doing something for the last time, and that one day we may look back longingly.

I hope you enjoy your childhood, and your teenage years, and early adulthood, and so on. They are each unique and special. And, if you aren't enjoying a certain phase in your life, take comfort, even if just a tiny bit of comfort, in knowing it is only temporary. Everything is temporary. In the words of my beloved Papa, *"Nothing forever."*

FAMILIES

Families do things differently. Each family has its own customs, values, traditions, languages, and beliefs. I think one part of growing up is coming to realize how the way your family "did things" is not how all families "did things." Perhaps even more importantly, there is no "normal" – every way is beautiful and unique. I saw this particularly after having Lily. Jamie and I, especially at first, came to see how we were acting as parents in ways that felt comfortable and familiar to us, and were just starting out in our journey to grow together as parents and feel our way into how we intentionally wanted to be as parents. We're each shaped by our own backgrounds. Your, my, anyone's way is not necessarily the "best" way. There is no best way. We must accept and embrace people for exactly who they are, and exactly who they are not.

Another thought on families – a family is a group of people who love each other and care for and support one another, sometimes connected by blood and heart, and sometimes connected only by heart. Some families have a mom, some have a dad, others have two moms or two dads, or any other combination under the sun. All of these combinations are wonderful and perfect.

THE STATUS QUO

I once heard (credit to Father Richard Rohr) that as humans, we are all addicted to the status quo, even when it's killing us. This really struck me as being true: this is how much the status quo is engrained in us. I think one of the most dangerous phrases is "we've always done it this way." I want to encourage you to always look to challenge the status quo – ask yourself: how can we make the world better? How can we make it more just? How can we create positive change? Social progress, over history, was only ever achieved through the brave and decisive actions of women and men who refused to accept the status quo, and who believed their vision of the future was not only possible, but within their reach.

Challenging the status quo may, you must be aware, come at a cost. Some people have lost their jobs, others have lost their lives. Sometimes, challenging the status quo can feel like getting into trouble: certain people won't like it and will try to tell you to "behave." The deceased U.S. Congressman John Lewis called this getting into "good trouble." He said, when reflecting on the state of racial inequality in the United States, that he was, in fact, inspired to get into good trouble. Good trouble is when you see something not right, not fair, or not just and you do something about it. I remember a few years ago when this happened to me: I was called to a partner's office and so I went, perhaps naively believing I was going to be thanked for my efforts on a recent gender equality initiative at my firm. Instead, he told me not to do what I did, how I did it, again. I was in trouble! I walked back to my office, tears brimming, feeling utterly demoralized. *Why did I bother?* I thought. It was later that night when I received the guidance I needed – Hillary Clinton in her concession speech, saying to all of us, "Never stop believing that fighting for what's right is worth it." It is always worth it.

And if you need a little spark to get yourself going, or overcome any feelings of fear or nervousness, especially if you feel like you may get into (good) trouble, ask yourself: what are you preserving the status quo at the expense of?

Remember, too, that there is an internal status quo. This is also known as our comfort zone. It's said that that we are at our happiest when we are just outside our comfort zone and still thriving. I also learned that being "stuck" – such as not making a decision one way or another – can lead to negative mental states, like psychosis. Do your best to avoid analysis paralysis (meaning, analyzing a decision for so long that it stops you from making a move). The important thing is to make a decision. Nothing is permanent. You can always choose another choice.

TRUSTING YOURSELF

You, and you alone, know what's "best" for you – what will make you feel light, bring you peace, fill you up energetically, give you faith you're on a soul-aligned path. You must always go inward to discover for yourself what is best for you, guided by your heart, mind, and intuition. My sister Kristen shared with me a beautiful quote by Johann Wolfgang von Goethe that perfectly captures this sentiment, which I will paraphrase as this: *"Once you trust yourself, you will know how to live."*

The story I want to share in this context is about when Jamie and I were getting married. It was November, a couple of months into living in Hong Kong, and we knew in our hearts how right it was for us, both the timing of getting married and the way we wanted to do it (over Christmas vacation, on the beach in Fiji, barefoot, just the two of us). Family asked us to wait and have a traditional wedding at a later date after we got back to the UK. It was a very challenging time, wanting the blessing of our families *and* wanting to still have our dream come true. After many emotional conversations, and after changing course and agreeing to wait, we took some breathing space to think deeply about it. One morning, we received the clarity we were praying for: getting married at that time is what we really wanted and what we felt was right for us. We trusted ourselves to move forward on this path. We spoke to family again, and this time, I believe because, energetically, we were coming from a place of pure clarity and peace, our family gave their blessing. A few weeks later, we said our vows, sea water gently lapping near us, and danced to our wedding song *It Feels Like Home* on the sand. Nothing had ever been so magical for us.

PAST RELATIONSHIPS

In case you ever get to a point where you feel like you "wasted time" in past relationships, please remember that nothing, ever, was "wasted time." There is a beauty and an intrinsic value in every relationship. You also learn something from every relationship, including about yourself. And what's more, with every relationship that ends, you are also that much closer to knowing what you want and need in a partner (if having a partner is something you seek).

SEE THE WORLD

Travel as much as you can! Explore the world and its many wonders. Spend time and have adventures in other towns, cities, countries; definitely live in different parts of the world if you can. There is a something extraordinarily special about going to experience a place and its people with your own senses, and even more special getting to live among them. This expands your mind and your heart, and your capacity to connect with and understand and appreciate others. It also pushes you outside your comfort zone, which is very important, and makes you realize how what you think is "normal" is nothing more than your own perceptions based on your own life experiences.

The weekend after I had left the United States for the first time, in January 2007, when I was studying abroad at Oxford University during college, we went on an adventure weekend in West Wales. One of our activities was coasteering – wearing thick wetsuits, we climbed cliffs and then jumped into the sea. I had never felt a feeling of exhilaration like that before, or since. I remember looking out to the horizon and at the water all around me thinking, "I am in the Irish Sea!" A whole new world opened up to me. I wrote in my journal shortly after that, *"The more of the world I see, the more of the world I want to see."* This sentiment has never left me. I hope the same for you.

SEEK DIVERSITY

Surround yourself with people different to you – seek diversity in all forms. Seek out different perspectives and experiences. Listen to them. Learn from them. Value them. This is one way to strengthen your empathy and compassion for others. As my sister Kristen and her daughter, my five-year-old niece Brooke, tell each other, *"Different is special."* May we today, and always, celebrate the diversity of human creation and experience.

YOGA

Yoga has a drastically wonderful impact on your body and mind. I love how each time you do yoga, you create a tiny, often imperceptible, shift in your body; those tiny shifts add up, in time, to seemingly miraculous changes. A few years ago, for example, before I started doing yoga and would mainly run as my form of exercise, I didn't think I'd be able to touch my toes while standing up. Now, I can put my hands flat on the ground. Every time I do it, I feel so strong and in total awe of my body.

Another little memory: a yoga teacher I had in Hong Kong was talking, toward the end of class, about her daughter. I was pregnant at this point and I assumed, looking at her youthful body, that she was early 30s, like me. She then said she was 54 (!) and started doing yoga when she was 28. This certainly inspired me to keep my yoga practice going.

LOVING YOUR BODY

Your body is miraculous, and I hope you never spend a moment wishing it were different to exactly the way it is. I realized this fully only after giving birth. My body created, and carried, and brought into the world, and then wholly sustained another human being. Our bodies are incredible for what they are capable of, and perfect just the way they are.

I will also say that I think I am like many women in disliking my hair for a lot of my life. I straightened it, bleached it, dyed it, and generally treated it disrespectfully. Just before Lily was born, I cut off the remaining light blonde bits, which had long grown out. I was, for the first time in many years, back to being a strawberry blonde, and I let it go naturally curly, without so much as using a hairdryer. It took a long time, and a lot of emotional moments, to get to that place of what felt like reclaiming my natural self and freedom. As my friend Frida had said, our natural features (like my natural hair color) are designed for us and therefore suit us. If you are ever in a similar feeling about your hair, or any other natural feature, I pray you too find your way to self-love.

"BAD" WEATHER

A few months ago, I heard for the first time that *"there is no bad weather, only bad clothing."* I love this. It made me embrace the idea, especially in a long, dark, wet London winter, of putting on waterproof over-clothes and going out to play and dance in that rain. Or, forget the waterproof over-clothes and go anyway. My heart always delights in seeing little toddlers splashing in rain puddles; they are not perturbed by the inevitable sogginess but rather rejoice in the fun of it all. It is so wonderful, and inspiring.

SAVING

My mom used to say to me when I was growing up, "What are you saving it for?" In other words, life is short, you may as well enjoy something now. This mindset took on a new life for me during my maternity leave, which was during the global coronavirus pandemic. For many people, me included, we no longer took for granted certain things we did in the past; life felt a lot more fragile, uncertain, and precious. At that time I saw a quote which said, *"Never save anything for a special occasion; being alive is the special occasion."* This deeply resonated with me. When tragedy and sadness and sorrow were all around us, it made me remember so fundamentally how being alive – just being alive – was something to be celebrated and cherished. That night I opened the bottle of champagne I had been "saving" for me and Jamie to enjoy. We toasted to life.

SEX

When it comes to sex, do what you feel comfortable doing. Say "no" to what you don't feel comfortable doing. Don't worry about someone else's feelings in this regard. If you decide to have sex, take precautions and be safe.

Don't feel like you need to do anything sexual because you owe it to anyone. You owe it to no one. No matter what they did for you, or under any circumstance.

Also, if you have sex with someone you end up no longer liking, it's okay. It's okay! There is nothing wrong with having multiple sexual partners. You are not "loose" or "sinful" or any other derogatory term you may hear. You can explore sex in the same way you explore all other aspects of your life and yourself.

INTENTION

In life, it is vitally important that you remember to continually check in with yourself and ask yourself, *"What is my intention?"* Your intention is what underlies all of your actions. When you ask yourself what is your intention, and when you're fully honest with yourself about it, you will find clarity as to why you are doing what you are doing, which can also be a powerful motivating or guiding force. You may also realize that your *actual* intention was hidden from your view, which can realign you or clear up an inner confusion or conflict you may be having.

At times when I was writing this book, and feeling vulnerable and also afraid of judgment, I would bring myself back to my intentions. I would remind myself that my intention was about showing up as the person I want to be in the world: for Lily to know I wrote a book for her and all daughters, for myself to know I did what I set out to do, and to be a force for good in the world to raise money in aid of women and children who face domestic violence. By bringing myself back to my intentions, I could override my feelings of doubt and fear, and keep on this path.

CAREER

There is an expression that "*if you do something you love, you'll never work a day in your life.*" I learned a few months ago that finding your "element" (credit to Ken Robinson) is when what you love doing intersects with what you're good at doing. Many find their element with their career, and others do their career in order to be able, in their leisure time, to find their element. Both options are great.

There are an infinite number of things you could do for your career. Follow your curiosity and what interests you. You may decide to choose a career you love which pays little, or one you hate which pays a lot. Or some mixture of these. Remember, there are trade-offs and no right way. Everyone must choose for themselves.

If you take a job that doesn't fulfill you, though, for certain other reasons, such as needing the money to repay education loans, consider this advice (thanks to Wes Moore) that you should leave the job the moment you feel you can leave; every moment you stay longer than you feel you have to, you will become extraordinarily ordinary.

Consider this: working hard for something you don't care about = stress. But, working hard for something you love = passion.

BRAVERY

Being brave doesn't mean you don't feel fear; it means you still *go for it*, even despite the fear. In the words of Susan Jeffers, you feel the fear, and do it anyway. The fear becomes something you move through. Sometimes, you must just take a deep breath, call on the divine guidance and support of the universe, and act. This is how you build the bravery muscle. Remember the proverb which says, *"fortune favors the bold."* In other words, courageous action is often rewarded. It is bravery that propels us forward into new realms and domains.

Also remember how Dr. Maya Angelou called courage the most important of all the virtues. This is because without courage, you cannot practice any other virtue consistently. I believe being brave is a virtue because it enables us to show up in our lives as who we truly are and who we can be for others.

Lastly, remember Malala Yousafzai's response to being asked whether she is "brave" (she was shot in the head by the Taliban for advocating for education for girls): *"For me, bravery is when you speak up and speak out for what is right, and it's our responsibility. It's not that we do something – give something extra – and do a favor to our community. I think it's our duty and we should do it and we must do it."* I hope, like me, you will always remember these wisest of words, especially in times you feel scared or stuck. Choose to be brave – it is your duty.

There is one caveat about fear, in this context, that I must mention. Sometimes, we may feel what feels like fear – like a feeling that something is wrong. Take care that this may not be fear, but actually is an intuition. Something may, in fact, be wrong. You may be sensing a dark energy or a dangerous presence. In these moments, you also act. You get yourself to a place of safety. And you do not worry about being polite along the way.

PLAY

When we are little, play is an inextricable part of our being. Our imaginations are huge. Months ago, I walked by two little girls playing in the park. One said to the other, "Okay let's not be normal – let's have magical powers." And off they ran. It brought back such beautiful memories from my childhood, like playing Barbies in our basement with my sister Kristen, where we'd spend hours and hours acting out different storylines, stopping only when we were told it was bedtime.

As we get older, and are increasingly faced with the "reality" of adulthood, I think we can often forget about the importance of play. As Brené Brown says, play is time spent without purpose. Play brings you pleasure. Being playful keeps you feeling young and alive. I encourage you, throughout your life, to find those activities which feel like play, where you are doing it solely for the enjoyment it brings you. For me, it's swimming; when I'm in a pool or in the sea, I suddenly feel an overwhelming feeling of "childlike" fun and delight, and like I never want to leave. When I was pregnant with Lily, Jamie and I went on a "babymoon" to Cyprus where each day I'd spend most of the day swimming in the warm, clear water, feeling like a fish. I could see how nourishing it was for my soul to have a few days of play.

I encourage you to try a lot of things. Find what you enjoy, and make time, as one of your priorities, to play. Remember the words of George Bernard Shaw: "We don't stop playing because we grow old; we grow old because we stop playing."

BECOMING A PARENT

Becoming a parent is the best thing I have ever done – even despite the undeniable exhaustion, and sometimes the feelings of rage and like I want to escape! For me, there is no feeling like the feeling I get when kissing Lily's soft cheek. Or seeing Lily smile and giggle. After spending the entire day with Lily, when Jamie is taking her up the stairs for a bath, and Lily is looking at me like "Where am I going, Mommy?" I already start to miss holding her. I am privileged and honored to be Lily's mom.

I am sharing this, and at the same time acknowledging that you may decide that being a parent is not for you, and I honor your choice. This is something so wholly personal, and something every person must determine for themselves.

DIFFERING OPINIONS

I learned a simple, beautiful phrase to use when you do not agree with someone about something. It is respectful, civil, and perfectly clear. I have loved using it, in its exact formulation, since I learned of it. It removes any hostility or animosity, and doesn't suggest that the other person is wrong or that you are right, which wards off unnecessary argument. Here it is (thank you to Sister Joan Chittister): "I think differently about that." That's it. I think often when we disagree with someone, there is a tendency to feel a conflict or like we're in combat. Remember that nothing is "wrong" when we have a differing opinion; we can acknowledge the differing opinion openly and respectfully.

CONFIDENCE

I learned during my maternity leave, thanks to Susie Moore, that confidence is nothing more than being willing to experience a possible "negative" emotion, such as embarrassment. In other words, you put yourself out there with the knowledge that you will be absolutely fine, whatever happens. You are at peace, for example, with the idea that someone may disagree with you, or decide not to engage with you in the way you hoped, or not say anything back to you at all. When you have confidence in yourself, you take heart in knowing you have good intentions and you do not need to control the outcome or another person's reaction or response to you. This is true confidence that comes from within and radiates out.

BACK STORIES

Everyone has a back story. What is a back story? It's what you don't see on social media, which is carefully curated. I learned this, in particular, during my maternity leave when I posted on Facebook about how difficult a time I was having as a mom around the time Lily was four months old – I was exhausted, my body hurt, I wished I had more help. (This was also likely exacerbated by it being during the global pandemic.) Many friends, from many stages of my life, reached out to me to say things like they totally understood what I was going through, or to offer kind solidarity and support. It was wonderful to reconnect with so many old friends as our new selves as moms.

One old friend from college confided that during those early times with her first child, she and her husband used to get into shouting matches that were so bad, one time he slammed the front door and she thought he was leaving her. All I ever remember seeing on her social media feeds were the happiest of photos, like the happiest family you've ever seen. And I suddenly got it: she is me, and she is all of us. We generally put onto social media the best times, not the worst. The smiling photo captures one snapshot. You know what it does not reveal? The back story. So, remember to always have compassion for others. You might not know the full picture of their lives.

MARRIAGE

I want to encourage you not be in a rush to get married (if marriage is something you want). Life is so long and it's a gift to have the time and space to grow and develop as a whole person before undertaking a commitment to someone else. We are continually evolving beings and our energy is always interacting with others' energy.

I also want to share that in the few years I have been married, I have continued to learn what an evolving relationship and dynamic it is. I have learned that you grow together as a couple, and also grow separately. It is important to maintain your separate sense of self, so you are each a whole person contributing to your relationship. The person you are married to may not always show up as the perfect person you want them to be, and that is okay. Give yourselves grace to be who you each are.

Also, please know that marriage is whatever you and the person you're married to create it to be. Try to resist getting bogged down in societal or cultural expectations or norms of marriage. Like everything else in your life, you can create whatever marriage (or other relationship) you desire and dream of and is right for you. There are no rules except for your rules.

WEDDINGS

Remember that getting married is different from and separate to having a wedding. If a day comes when you choose to get married and choose to have a wedding, do what feels right to you and the person you're marrying. It's the day you and the person you're marrying are committing to each other – that can be as intimate or public as you'd like. The day is about you and your love.

SLEEP

Sleep as much as you can. Your body and brain will love it. When I first became a mom, I was told that, whenever I have an opportunity to sleep, sleep like I won't sleep for the next three years. I found this to be excellent advice, as it was creating a reserve I would later need to draw on.

When I was younger, I used to live by the motto, in half marathons as in life, *"run as fast as you can in any moment, and don't worry about how tired you'll be later."* While I see why I felt this way at that time, I can also now see, in hindsight, that this was a way I was burning myself out. With loving compassion, I would say to my younger self after you're finished running the half marathon, or working the all-nighter, or staying out very late with friends, make sure to take time to rest, sleep, and nourish yourself back to neutral.

And if you can't sleep, relax. Take a deep breath and relax.

"MODESTY"

I learned a beautiful quote that there is nothing arrogant in sharing your light. In fact, it's the opposite – it is generous and kind to share your light, meaning, for example, your skills and strengths and your own communication of your skills and strengths. I believe a lot of girls and women are taught or conditioned to "downplay" themselves, including their skills and strengths. There are many reasons for this, many are rooted in patriarchal societal norms in which girls and women are expected to accommodate boys and men. Similarly, I read from Bethany Webster that the best gift you can give to others is showing them how your life is working. Don't feel you need to hide the good in your life. You can inspire others through your example.

There is one nuance I want to mention. I saw a post on LinkedIn which said *"Be the kind of woman who makes other women want to up their game"* – except, the words *"want to up their game"* were crossed out and replaced with *"feel worthy regardless of how their game is going."* I think this is a very important message. When you put yourself out there, in sharing your achievements for example, think how to do so in a way which embraces others and brings others with you on your journey in our collective human experience. Ask yourself, how can you share yourself in a way that lifts other people up with you?

CURIOSITY

Be curious about everyone you meet: everyone you meet knows more about something than you. Everyone has something to teach you. I love this advice I learned this year from Elizabeth Gilbert: "follow your curiosity." If you don't know what your passion is in order to follow it, that's totally fine: just follow your curiosity instead. Your curiosity will lead you on many adventures and to many endeavors. As Albert Einstein once said: *"I have no special talents. I am only passionately curious."*

YOU ARE WORTHY

You are worthy, exactly as you are. You do not need to do anything *to try* to be worthy or to try to prove your worth. You do not need to gather up a lot of accomplishments to prove your worth.

I recently saw something from Cathy Heller which shifted how I think about this: *"The biggest way we block our desires is by not believing we are worthy of them."* Wow. This really made me consider how I may be blocking my desires subconsciously. Please know, for sure, you are worthy of anything and everything you desire.

WORK TO BE PROUD OF YOURSELF

Please be guided by doing what would make you proud of yourself. This is far more important that doing something to make your parents, or anyone else, proud. I want you to be guided from within, from that place inside you which feels you are aligned with your own values and dreams and desires.

VALIDATION

It is part of our collective human experience that we all want to be validated, we all want to be seen, and we all want to know that we matter. In other words, every human seeks validation; it's a basic human instinct. Validation, therefore, is a gift you can give to others: showing up for someone and showing them that they have been seen and have been heard. Be present and give someone space to share with you, to be with you, and to be themselves with you. If you don't know what else to say to someone, simply say this, "I hear you, and I am here with you."

THE POINT OF LIFE

You are here to learn and you are here to heal. Every experience and person in your life is here to teach you something. I believe, which is something I have come to believe based on what I've learned in the time since Lily was born, is that we are all spiritual beings here having a human experience. This means that our soul is eternal and will live on and reincarnate into different human lives after our current human life is over. I believe our soul has therefore created this human shell and personality in order to learn and heal whatever it is our soul needs to learn and heal.

When something unwelcome or terrible happens, or you find yourself needing to interact with someone you find triggering or unpleasant, ask yourself, *"What is this (or this person) here to teach me?"* Maybe it's patience. Maybe it's compassion. Maybe it's that you need to stop trying to control an outcome. Asking yourself this question can be very difficult to do, and can push us to our psychological limits, but I encourage you to always try to ask this and search your heart and mind for the answer.

GET MOVING

If you ever feel "stuck" mentally, get moving. Moving your body, especially outside in fresh air, can do wonders for you mentally in terms of getting feelings and thoughts flowing in and out of you. For me, I get this from running. I never regret going for a run. Once I'm in the flow of a run, new thoughts and ideas and inspirations form in my mind in a way I know they wouldn't otherwise. I encourage you to give this a try, in whatever way feels authentic to you.

SELF-RESPECT

Always be guided by respect for yourself. This is a foundational pillar of your humanhood. Do not be *respectful* of someone else at the expense of *respecting* yourself. To respect yourself, I believe, this means you must listen to, value, trust, and be considerate to yourself. I learned that at times, for example, I was taking into account other people's desires and wishes without also asking myself what felt good and right to me. You respect yourself by also asking and considering what feels good to you.

SURRENDERING

Feel free and relaxed in surrendering your desires to the universe. The universe is here to help and support you. To paraphrase the wisdom from Paulo Coelho, when you desire something, the universe conspires to help you achieve it. There is an energetic shift from the moment you determine what your desire is and release it.

Toward the end of my maternity leave, and after much emotional uncertainty, I surrendered two important things to the universe: a new job for myself that aligns to my values and "new" life as a mom, and a new home that provides comfort and space for my family. For one of these, following advice by Gabrielle Bernstein, I wrote it on a piece of paper and, one morning while holding Lily in my arms, buried it in dirt in my backyard. I did the work – searched and applied for the jobs, searched and viewed the houses – and left the rest up to the universe. In gratitude and grace, I share that I am soon starting the new job that inspires me, and we are now living in the new house that we love.

PARENTS

A usual refrain is that a parent "tried their best." This may definitely be true. But please remember that this does not mean that a parent is infallible. A parent's best may have had unconstructive impacts. You may decide you disagree with some of the ways you were parented, and that is okay! You are your own person with your own unique combination of preferences, desires, and values. You have a right to use your voice and express your opinion. We are all works in progress and, I hope, committed to learning and growing throughout our entire lives.

DIVORCE

There is a narrative in society that divorce is a terrible thing, like on par with death. I don't believe it has to be this way, or should be. I believe, even with the best of intentions, a marriage may end, and that is okay. Put another way, one person (or both people) may choose to end a marriage, and that is okay. There is also no shame in divorce. There, instead, can be a tremendous amount of love and compassion in freeing and releasing someone back into the world, if that is what they want, and even if it is sad or painful.

I love the conception of a relationship as described by Gary Zukav as a "spiritual partnership": this is a relationship of equals formed by two people for the purpose of, and who are as equally committed to, the evolution of their own soul as the other person's soul. They love each other very much, are on a journey together, and believe that if the time comes when their souls are finished evolving together, they will move on from each other in grace and gratitude. Remember, too, that something doesn't have to last forever for it to be meaningful.

POWER OF THE SISTERHOOD

Never underestimate what you can accomplish by harnessing the power of fellow women. If you need inspiration, think of Leymah Gbowee, author of *Mighty Be Our Powers*. With persistence, determination, and limitless grit, she unified and mobilized masses of disparate women, all envisioning a better life for Liberia's children, in order to bring peace to Liberia. The power of their sisterhood was so mighty that they, ultimately, ended a war. Just imagine what else the power of the sisterhood is capable of.

OUR WORLD

Our world needs us. Our planet is in trouble. I watched a sobering David Attenborough documentary which painted a bleak picture of the future of Earth, unless drastic action is taken. I want to please, please encourage you to find ways to do whatever you can to help preserve the many diverse species of life on Earth.

ACTUAL PHONE CALLS

This may in the future, or even now, sound "old-fashioned." My wish is that you will call friends on your phone to talk in real time, not just text them or communicate in delayed ways. Whenever a friend calls you, answer it. It's a blessing to have a friend who wants to speak to you. I read a story once of how humans are losing their ability to speak to one other in real life, as we grow increasingly accustomed to being able to think, type, edit, type again, send. There is no substitute for a live chat. This is how we form real connection. Often, even just one conversation can leave an imprint of a memory which lasts forever.

HARD WORK

As my Papa used to say in his Croatian-accented English, "Hard work killed nobody." He moved to the United States when he was 35. Not speaking English. No job. With my Nana (aged 32) and their eleven-year-old daughter (my mom). He would often tell me of their life in America, especially at first. He worked one job chipping ice and putting it into bags, for a quarter a piece. He also made sandwiches at a deli. He worked his way to become a cook, and then a chef. He did every job with pride, to survive, and to create a life for his family better than that which he had known. He would often tell me how lucky I was to have my job (as a corporate lawyer), and I would nod sincerely in agreement. Hard work creates strong character. I want to encourage you to take the mentality that no job is beneath you. Roll up your sleeves, and dive in.

BABIES

Having a baby is hard work. Hard, hard work. You fight exhaustion constantly. Exhaustion plays tricks with your mind, specifically your mental well-being. It can make lovely things bleak. It can make you question your sanity. If you become a mom, remember this: ask for help if you can. Share your struggles open and honestly. This is for the greater good of all moms everywhere, as well as yourself.

As I write this, Lily is eight months old, though when I started this section, Lily was a few months younger. It's already fading for me the memory of the exhaustion of which I wrote.

And now as I write this, Lily is ten months old, and again the exhaustion has continued to fade. It is the strangest experience of wanting these days to pass and never wanting these days to pass.

CREATIVITY

Creativity is about bringing into the world that which does not yet exist. We each possess an innate creativity, and it manifests in its own unique way. (For me, I believe it is through writing, such as this book.) Let your creativity shine through your own experimentation of what feels natural to you. When you are expressing yourself creatively, in a way that resonates with you, will often feel like you are in a state of flow. This will lead to brilliant contributions you will offer to the world.

BREAK DOWNS

By break downs, I mean times in your life when things aren't working as you'd want them to. You will face tough times; we all do. Try to think of them as storms – they will pass. My Nana would go one step further and say to go dance in that rain; it means that new sunshine is to follow.

Someone recently told me how every challenge we face is an opportunity to learn and, once we adopt this mindset, we're more likely to bounce back from lows and less likely to freeze once we step out of our comfort zone. Life can sometimes seem like a rollercoaster with an ongoing and never-ending series of highs and lows, break downs and breakthroughs. One quote I always try to remember (thanks to my leadership seminar leader Jatin) is, *"What comes next after a breakthrough? A break down. But what comes next after a break down? A breakthrough."*

In life, we need periods of volatility and uncertainty as much as we need periods of stability and equilibrium. This keeps us growing as humans, and adds a vibrancy, rather than stagnation, to our lives. Even if you are going through what feels like a long period of break down, one day, keep faith, you will emerge from the cocoon as a new butterfly on a new Earth.

Also remember that despite a break down or a tough time, you do not need to feel like you are suffering. Suffering means wishing whatever is happening is not happening. If you "accept" what is happening is happening, you will suffer less. From another perspective, this one from Viktor E. Frankel, if you feel that suffering is unavoidable, it may cease the moment you can identify a meaning, a purpose, for the suffering. You must discover this for yourself.

OUR STORIES

I want to pass on something life-changing that I learned a few years ago. Be very aware that there is a huge distinction between "the things that happened in our lives" and "the *stories* we have about the things that happened in our lives." We often collapse the two, with our "stories" – meaning, all the meaning and editorializing we did about what happened, as well as our feelings about what happened – overpowering what *actually* happened – meaning, just the objective facts. When our stories overpower what actually happened, it is the story that can remain with us and impact us, often negatively, for many years, possibly forever if we're not conscious to it. For example, the thing that happened was that someone broke up with you; the story you have about what happened is that you weren't good enough; and the impact on you, as a result of that story, is a fear that the next person you date may break up with you too because you aren't good enough.

Through life, as humans we tend to continue to pick up these stories – about ourselves, about others, about the way the world "is" and "isn't." One usual consequence is that we then get stuck, feeling we are fixed as people. Thinking, I am *this* or I am *that*. We, in other words, get stuck in our stories.

You must do the work to recognize what are the stories you have which are playing out in your life. Remember, in this context, if you are feeling stuck in your stories, that you are not static. You are capable of growth at any time, at any age, in any circumstance. With a growth mindset, rather than a fixed mindset, you are capable of anything, capable of creating all possibilities in your life. You are whoever you say you are. No one else has a right to define you or label you or put you into certain boxes.

LISTENING TO YOUR LIFE

As Oprah says, your life is always speaking to you. As you go through life, learn to be receptive to the guidance that comes your way – nudging you one way or another. I believe this guidance comes from the universe, God, your higher consciousness, your guardian angel or archangel, or spirit guides, or any combination of these. You may see signs or synchronicities. As my friend Holland says, *"coincidences are God's way of staying anonymous."*

OPTIONS

As people, we often have it like we have no options – we "have" to do this, or we "need" to do that. You always – always – have options. Even when you think you don't have options, you have options. The feeling of having no options often results from feeling powerless or because the options you do have are difficult ones. Remember, options are not always easy, but that does not mean they aren't there. And sometimes you need to choose the difficult option, not because you want to or because you're not afraid, but because you know in your heart and soul it's the right option.

APPRECIATION

You cannot over-appreciate someone. You, equally, cannot over-thank someone. Appreciate the people in your life and thank them as often as you can. Tell people what you've appreciated from them. Feeling appreciation is another way of feeling gratitude, and being in this feeling is a way to make you feel wonderful, high vibration energy. A fun exercise I learned from Gabrielle Bernstein is the Appreciation Game, which not too long ago helped me and Jamie out of an annoyance with each other. I started, and told Jamie one thing I appreciate about him. He quickly replied with one thing he appreciates about me. We repeated this again. By the end of the third round, I had a tear in my eye and our agitation toward each other melted entirely to love. We kissed and finished our dinner filled with peace. Another exercise I recently learned is to start every morning – the moment you are awake – with mentally creating a list of five things in your life that you are grateful for. This creates your energy for the day.

One more thing. Sometimes it's easy to slip into feeling like we would be more appreciative of things in our lives if we had more – if, if, if. The quote I always like to think about here is the one that goes, I cried because I had no shoes until I met a man who had no feet. The moral? Rather than focus on what you don't have, appreciate what you do have.

CONNECTION

One of the most beautiful things about being alive is the ability to connect to other human beings. Show yourself. Let others share with you. Connecting with a stranger feels so, so good. The person sitting next to you on an airplane. (I know someone who met her husband that way.) Your taxi driver. (I've lost count of the valuable life advice they've given me.) The girl you met on a night out. (She could become one of your most trusted confidants.) You never know.

What's particularly incredible is connecting with someone from a different background or culture or country. When I used to waitress at Carlucci's Italian Grill in New Jersey, most of my colleagues were from Latin America and spoke Spanish with a little English. I was the opposite – English with a little Spanish. I remember so vividly the sweetest memories of all of us standing around sharing in a laugh together over something that we all found funny – despite the language and cultural barriers. I was a high school student, many of them were in their 20s and 30s. We didn't have particularly much in common. But working together in high stress, close quarters created great bonds. It felt almost like a family, and I always felt lucky to have a chance to get to know people with different lives to me. I hope for you to create many opportunities like this.

IMPOSSIBILITY

When you are told something is "impossible" (or can't be done or has never been done before), remember this, as shared by my friend Charlotte: *"everything was impossible until someone did it."*

I loved learning about author Buchi Emecheta, whose novel *Second-Class Citizen* I read during my maternity leave. She was a mother who, after leaving her husband, obtained an honors degree in sociology while supporting her five children and writing in the early morning. She dedicated *Second-Class Citizen* to her five children without whose background noises, she writes, the book would not have been written. Wow. She certainly inspired me that writing a book, even as a busy mom, is possible.

This also reminds me of how I read that the actress Laverne Cox, a transgender woman, and the first transgender person to be nominated for an Emmy Award, prefers to be known as a "possibility model" (rather than a role model). What an exquisite phrase. Someone first does the "impossible" and suddenly, and forever, it is something that is possible.

ASKING

There is never harm in asking – anyone for anything. Don't be afraid of hearing no. Also, don't be afraid of hearing yes.

One story: it was my first time leaving Lily for an extended period of time when I went into central London for a hospital appointment. Lily was still breastfeed and I felt nervous being away from her. (Lily was, no doubt, safe and happy at home with Jamie. These were likely my own insecurities.) As I arrived at the waiting room, my heart sank when I saw there were two other people at my timeslot. During my pre-operation chat with the surgeon, she informed me I would be second to be operated on. I thought to myself, "Why not ask?" I asked the surgeon if it would it be possible to be first and told her the reason was that it was my first time away from my baby and I'd like to get home to her as soon as possible, but I understood if not. She said, without hesitation, it was no problem; none of us were emergency cases, and the order was just random. I breathed a sigh of relief, and later that day got home at what felt like just in time for an afternoon milk feed and nap.

Remember to ask. We get in life what we ask for.

KEEPING A JOURNAL

Keep a journal. Write as often as you can. You will love to look back on your life through your own words. I started keeping a journal in fourth grade, just as my family was soon to move from New York to New Jersey. I was inspired by something I had read in class: *"Remember your past: your memories do add up."* I distinctly remember writing at the desk in my bedroom, reflecting on the big change about to happen to me, working out my big feelings on paper.

It has always felt like a new life chapter starting, or ending, a journal. My last journal I started the day Lily was born, euphorically writing from my hospital bed as she slept. Trying to put my emotions onto paper. Trying to capture how I felt, what had just happened, how awe-struck I was with this little tiny human who somehow was my daughter.

A few months ago, my parents mailed me my collection of diaries I still had at their house. I had bundled them together in an ordinary box, whose purpose I had long forgot, but which fit all of them perfectly, like a 3D jigsaw puzzle. As soon as I received the large package, I ripped it open, like I was discovering treasure. I tore through my diaries one by one, starting with my first one, barely able to stop for sleep. *So this is who I was*, I kept thinking to myself, as I read. I was struck by so many things. By how young I once sounded. By my teenage obsession with boys (most of whom didn't seem to like me back). By the importance of friends in my life. By how amazing I sounded at 19 – so vibrant and confident, ready to take on the entire world.

My diaries brought back for me so much richness, so many details I had long forgotten. Your memories will fade. Not all of them, but many. Photos are great, too, but will not always be enough to capture your thoughts or how you were feeling in those moments. Reading your own thoughts from years past, you are reconnected with yourself in an incomparable way.

ADVICE

Be critical of all advice you are given (including mine!). Everyone gives their advice from their own perspective and experiences. *"We don't see the world as it is, we see it as we are,"* as Anaïs Nin said. To say that again, for you to really take it in: We see the world *as we are*. Everything is from our own (or someone else's) perception. So, sometimes advice can be a subconscious (or intentional) justification or rationalization of one's own life choices. This is very important: just because someone is by age older than you does not mean they know better than you, especially on the topic of what's best for you or what you "should" do. Don't be afraid to receive, or solicit, advice, but just know to apply your own filter, use your own brain, to consider it and decide whether and how to apply it to your life. If someone is insistent in what they're telling you, all you have to say is "Okay, thanks." That's it. You don't need to offer an explanation if you don't want to.

UNCERTAINTY

Life can at times feel uncertain. I think this was many people's experience especially during the pandemic. We as humans often search for and crave certainty. So when we don't feel we have certainty, about our path in life, for example, we can feel anxious or scared. If one day you find yourself feeling this way, I want you to remember something extremely important: the only certainty in life is… uncertainty. As humans we go around thinking that there is ever any certainty in life, when really there never is. I say this in order for you to embrace uncertainty. Uncertainty is life. We live each day, each moment, as it comes.

HOW YOU KNOW A RELATIONSHIP IS OVER

Trying to figure out whether to end a relationship, or whether to keep working at it, can feel really difficult. Should you try harder? Can you work some things out? Or, should you move on, and try to meet someone – who may or may not be out there – who is a better match for you?

I once sat in a fork in a road, literally on a bench in a small park in an actual fork in a road, with my then-boyfriend, trying to decide if we should stay together or not, looking for divine guidance. I looked around me at both streets of the fork thinking, *I see what you're telling me here, universe.* My brain felt so muddled; I think I felt scared and confused. We were due to be at my friend's wedding in one hour's time, and we couldn't decide if he should come with me, or just go home. I knew he was a good person and was objectively an excellent boyfriend; I also knew I was not liking who I was showing up as in our relationship, or feeling happy. We continued to churn and stew for a few more weeks until one lunch break, when I was out running along the Thames River on a beautiful crisp and sunny early autumn day, I felt calm and clear and knew this was the time. I called him and we had a straightforward conversation. No, we were no longer together. Yes, we wished each other well.

A few weeks later I met Jamie.

If you feel you want to get out of a relationship, give it due consideration. This could be a day, a week, an hour. Only you know – it's not about the time you spend, but how you feel. Try to listen to what your higher self is telling you. And sometimes take a leap of faith.

BE HERE NOW

If you find yourself feeling unsteady – uncertain about the future, anxious about the past – take yourself back to the present moment. This is how magical little kids' lives are. They have no conception of the future and no attachment to the past. Everything is what is currently unfolding before them. I remind myself of a simple phrase, passed onto me by my friend Holland, which often grounds me: "Be here now." Wherever your mind is taking you to, just gently nudge yourself back to the present moment with *be here now*. And then be with what is then around you – even as simple as the sun on your skin, the breath in your lungs, the sight of your hands.

PHOTO ALBUMS

I encourage you to make photo albums. I do not know if this advice will soon sound incredibly antiquated, but I want to encourage you to make hard copy photo albums (and not rely solely on digital albums). I think there is something magical about making them, and something even more magical in looking at them years later. As you go through life stages, it is hard to imagine that it won't always be this way. And then years, decades even, go by and it is because of photo albums that you are able to look back.

I am currently on Part 6 of the Jamie and Megan (and now Lily) series. I love to look back on Part 1 as Jamie and Megan, the new couple, running around London and Europe together as loved up pre-newlyweds. It was only a few years ago and when I look at the photos I see myself as a much younger version of myself, emotionally and spiritually, if not in age. I like to study our faces for clues as to how we felt in those moments.

The other day, I was looking at albums my mother-in-law made of photos from when she was a child. It was a rich tapestry – so many stories, so much history – that I already look forward to showing Lily one day.

BE KIND TO YOURSELF

There is a quote that says, *"of all the things you can be in this world, be kind."* I would also add to this, don't forget to be kind to yourself. Be as kind to yourself as you would be to your best friend. Give yourself grace. Grant yourself permission. Gift yourself patience. Sometimes you will be in a funk. Sometimes you will be stuck. Sometimes you will not feel content or at peace. These are all okay. Be okay to just be with yourself. The kindness you show for yourself will radiate to others.

WHAT OTHER PEOPLE THINK OF YOU

My friend Andrea passed on this perfect advice which I hope you remember too: *"What other people think of you is none of your business."* Try not to worry about, or even think about, what others may think of you. That is not your business. Stay, mentally and emotionally, in your own business. As Byron Katie teaches, there are only three kinds of business in the universe: your business, everyone else's business, and God's business. Staying in your own business, the only business you have control over, is how you set yourself free and prevent unneeded suffering.

MIRACLES

There is a beautiful quote from Albert Einstein, which I will paraphrase as this: *"there are two ways to live life: one is as if nothing is a miracle; the other is as though everything is."* I love the energy of this mindset – to live life, to look at all "ordinary" aspects of life all around us, as the truly miraculous and marvellous creations they are. Marianne Williamson teaches that a miracle is a shift from fear to love – from, for example, "Who am I to publish a book?" to "Who am I not to publish a book?" I hope you will carry this with you in all you do, seeing and creating miracles every day.

THE "RIGHT TIME"

I believe there is a cultural narrative that there is a "right time" to do something – and, therefore, also many wrong times. I saw a quote this year which shifted this belief for me. It says, "*There is no right time. There is only time, and what you do with it.*" In other words, the "right time" does not exist. All that exists is that you choose what you do when.

If you are feeling like it's not the "right time" to do something, ask yourself why not. What else may be going on which is blocking you? What is it you may be afraid of? How can you connect back to your intention or purpose? You may discover that now is *the* time. Now is *the only* time.

EXPRESSION

If you're going through a challenging time, or feeling some emotions we often label as negative, such as anger, or sadness, or fear, please share them with someone, like a trusted friend or a therapist. Express them to get them out of you. Often, getting out your feelings and thoughts can be like uncorking a bottle of bubbly liquid – once you remove the block, you are free to flow again.

Similar but different to therapy, expressing yourself to, and in turn receiving coaching from, a professional coach can push us to the version of ourselves that we can't yet see. I experienced this during my maternity leave with two coaches, Anya and Olivia, who, after giving me space to just simply express everything in my mind and heart, helped me to understand the importance of having and knowing one's purpose in life and helped me to identify and reconnect with what my purpose is, respectively. Working with a coach whose style and energy connects to yours can be truly life-changing.

AGE

Dr. Edith Eger published her first book (and the best book I ever read), *The Choice*, at 90. Last month, I read that a 70-year-old man rowed across the Atlantic Ocean alone in a boat called *Never Too Old*. Recently I saw a post on LinkedIn of a woman, smiling brightly with silver-blonde hair, holding a sign which read: "*Normalize finding love in your 40s. Normalize discovering and chasing dreams in your 30s. Normalize finding yourself and your purpose in your 50s. Life doesn't end at 25. Stop acting like it does.*" I hope and pray that I always embrace the following mindset, and that you do too: "*You're never too old and it's never too late.*"

I saw this beautifully first-hand at a personal development course I did a few years ago, through Landmark Worldwide. Many of the participants in the program were in their 20s through 40s, and nearly everyone was younger than retirement age. Much of the program involved participants going up to the microphone to share with the group their own experiences and anecdotes relating to the course material, all focused on transforming our lives for the better. At one point, a man got up to speak. He shared with us, relevant to the topic at hand, how he planned to implement what we were learning in his life going forward. He also shared, as an aside, that he was in his 80s. I remember feeling so inspired by him in that moment. He was creating a better future for himself, working to continue improving his life, *even* in his 80s.

If you ever feel like, for example, you want to change careers, or start a business, or move countries, and that it's "too late," please, please remember you are never too old and it is never too late. If, for example, you want to do something, such as go back to school to get a different degree, but worry that by the time you finish the course you'll be "X years old," remember that you will one day be "X years old" whether or not you do the thing you desire doing.

Remember there are no age limits on simple pleasures in life: kissing someone you fancy, building a sandcastle, eating an ice cream cone, dancing and singing your heart out. Age truly is only a number; you are only as old or young as you feel.

PROGRESS

I think we often think of "progress" as linear, all heading in a neat straight line. Remember that this simply isn't the case. Often, it is a squiggly line of lots of peaks and troughs. I hope for you to embrace the idea that what you are aiming for in life is progress, not perfection (credit to Marie Forleo). Saying this another way: take actions toward your goals, even if you aren't 100% sure about them or whether they will turn out as desired.

As Confucius said: *"It does not matter how slowly you go as long as you do not stop."* Any progress you make, in whatever form you can make it, is to be honored and celebrated. I felt this the other day as I completed one of my remaining maternity leave goals – to circumnavigate Richmond Park, in Southwest London, by bike. As I rounded one corner, toward the end of the 14 kilometer route, I was met with a steep hill which slowed my speed to barely a crawl. I felt tears welling as I painfully pushed one pedal, then another, feeling like every other cyclist was speeding past me. I thought in that moment of progress. No matter how long it took me, and even in my most unglamorous state, I would get to the top of that hill. I did, and I gleefully glided down the other side.

When you are contemplating quitting something you really desire, please think, too, of progress.

YOU

My final thought in this book is this: all you have is all you need. I saw a perfect quote, which said: *"You lack nothing. Use what I gave you. -God."* I love this so much. Imagine for a moment the truth of it! We all each possess exactly what we need. We are all each fully whole, infinitely capable, and uniquely ourselves.

AFTERWORD

A few months ago, in February, on what I can remember as one of the first sunny days after a long, seemingly endless grey London winter, I took Lily to a park by my house. As she snoozed in her stroller, I sat on a wooden bench, marvelling at the beautiful green grass before me and rejoicing in the sun rays on my face. It felt perfectly poetic. After so many months of darkness, in the season of nature and in my season as a new mom, Spring was here.

After Lily awoke, I began to follow her as she toddled in the direction of the playground. After a few steps, I looked back at the bench I had been sitting on, realizing it was dedicated to someone. Into the first piece of wood was carved her name and the years she lived. On the piece of wood below that, "*Lovely wife, loving mother, beloved grandmother.*" And on the piece of wood below that, "*Also: doughty school governor, phenomenal knitter, devoted gardener, resourceful BBC researcher, Lib Dem councillor for Sheen and Deputy Mayor of Richmond.*"

This made me think: what will be on my bench?

And now I ask you: what will be on your bench?

Your life is your own beautiful creation. Fill yourself up to the brim with possibility, love, and dreams. Your legacy will be the impact you made and the lives you touched.

Enjoy your life!

THANK YOU

Thank you for reading my thoughts and entrusting me with your time, energy, mind, and heart. Wherever you are in the world, awakened daughter, I am sending you love and light.

Megan Elizabeth Gray
London, April 2021

ABOUT THE AUTHOR

Megan Elizabeth Gray always wanted to live a life that means something for others and our world. This manifests in her career as a lawyer, in her family as a wife and mother, in her advocacy for women and gender equality, and in her passion for writing and sharing authentically. She is originally from New York, and has lived in London since graduating from Cornell Law School in 2011.

Printed in Great Britain
by Amazon